DISCOVERING LANGUAGES GERMAN

Elaine S. Robbins
Formerly Mount Logan Middle School
Logan, Utah

Kathryn R. Ashworth
Brigham Young University

When ordering this book, please specify R 592 S
or DISCOVERING LANGUAGES: GERMAN

AMSCO SCHOOL PUBLICATIONS, INC.
315 Hudson Street / New York, N.Y. 10013

To the memory of

Carl C. Robbins, Jr., beloved son and brother of the authors

Design and Production: Boultinghouse & Boultinghouse, Inc.

Cover Illustration: Delana Bettoli

Illustrations: Rick Brown, John R. Jones, Elise Mills, Ed Taber, George Ulrick

ISBN 1-56765-400-2
NYC Item 56765-400-1

Printed in the United States of America

4 5 6 7 8 9 10 02 01

To the Student

You are about to embark on a journey of discovery — beginning to learn a new language spoken by millions of people around the world, GERMAN.

Learning German provides an opportunity to explore another language and culture. German may be one of several languages you will discover in this course. You can then select which language you will continue to study.

Whatever your goals, this book will be a fun beginning in exploring a special gift you have as a human being: the ability to speak a language other than your own. The more you learn how to communicate with other people, the better you will be able to live and work in the world around you.

In this book, you will discover the German language and the world where it is spoken. The German words and expressions you will learn have been limited so that you will feel at ease.

You will learn how to express many things in German: how to greet people, how to count, how to tell the day and month of the year, how to identify and describe many objects, and more.

You will use German to talk about yourself and your friends. You will practice with many different activities, like puzzles and word games, German songs, fun cartoons, and pictures. Some activities you will do with classmates or with the whole class. You will act out skits and conversations and sing German songs. You will learn about many interesting bits of German culture: school days, holidays, school and leisure time, sports, and interesting manners and customs.

You will also meet young Udo, who will be your guide on how to pronounce German words. Look for Udo's clues throughout this book and get a feel for the German language, its sounds, and its musical quality. You will also develop an ear for German, so listen carefully to your teacher and the cassettes.

You will quickly realize that learning a new language is not as hard as you might have imagined. Enjoy using it with your teacher and classmates. Try not to be shy or afraid of making mistakes when speaking: remember, the more you speak, the more you will learn. And you can even show off the German you learn to family, relatives, and friends. After all, learning a new language means talking with the rest of the world and with each other.

Now — on to German. **Viel Glück!**, which means *Good luck!*

— *K.R.A.*

Contents

1 Germany and the German Language

Germany **(Deutschland),** slightly smaller than the state of Montana, is one of the largest countries in western Europe. Northern Germany is low and flat, sloping upwards to the central highlands and in the south to the Black Forest and the Bavarian Alps. The Rhine River, which flows through much of Germany, is the most important waterway in Europe. Germany has many other rivers and canals that form a network of water highways.

Bordered by eight neighboring countries on all sides, Germany has few natural boundaries. Its geographical location in the heart of the European continent has made it a historical arena for invasions and wars.

Throughout its history, Germany has been a united country only twice, from 1871 to 1945 and since 1990. After its defeat in World War II in 1945, Germany became once again a divided country. West Germany, which had been occupied by England, France, and the United States after the war, became democratic, and East Germany, which had been occupied by the Soviet Union, became communist. Berlin, the former national capital, was also divided between East and West. In 1990, the two Germanys were once more united and became the Federal Republic of Germany, with Berlin as its official capital.

The German language **(Deutsch)** is spoken by 120 million people. It is the official language of Germany, Austria, and Liechtenstein and one of the four official languages of Switzerland. German is also the first language of 300,000 people in Luxembourg and the mother tongue of millions of people in other European countries, the United States, Canada, and South America.

Modern German is one of the Germanic languages derived from the old Indo-European family of languages spoken three thousand to four thousand years ago in Central Europe. The German people are the descendants of various Germanic tribes that settled in Central and Northern Europe at least two thousand years ago.

The first writing in German dates from the eighth century. One form of German, Low German, developed in the low, northern plains. Low German has many similarities to Dutch, Flemish, and English, which are also Germanic in origin. Another form, High German, developed in the higher, southern part of the country. High German became the standard German used today. Two of the most important developments in the history of the German language were Johannes Gutenberg's invention of movable type for printing in 1440 and Martin Luther's translation of the Bible into High German in the sixteenth century.

Many German-speaking people took their language with them when they went to live in other parts of the world. For example, Yiddish is based on German dialects spoken in the Middle Ages by Jews who emigrated to eastern Europe and is still spoken by many of their descendants throughout the world today.

Germany has become famous for the achievements of its scientists and engineers. Over the centuries, Germany has also produced many great poets, writers, philosophers, and composers, whose works have won renown throughout the world. The cultural richness of Germany extends into the everyday life of its people. Germans love and practice many sports and enjoy celebrations of all kinds. They like rich, delicious foods, many of which — like sausage and beer — have become worldwide staples.

Unlike English, French, and Spanish, the German language did not spread through colonization. Rather, many people have learned German in order to be able to read, study, and enjoy the works of the many great thinkers who have written in that language. Because of their common origin, German and English have many words that are similar — even identical — to each other. Only their pronunciation differs. These similarities will help you as you begin to learn German.

ÜBUNG

1. In which part of Germany are the Black Forest and the Bavarian Alps?

   They are in the south

2. What is the Rhine?

3. When and why was Germany divided into West Germany and East Germany?

4. What is the official capital of Germany?

5. In which three countries of Europe is German the only official language?

6. In which European country is German one of four official languages?

7. When did writing develop in Germany?

8. Name four Germanic languages.

9. Why is the German from the southern part of Germany called High German?

10. Which two events were important to the history of the German language?

11. Name two famous food products of Germany.

2 German Cognates

You already know many German words. Some German words are spelled exactly like English words and have the same meanings: **Ball**, **Name**, **Hand**, **Sofa**, **warm**, **wild**. Many other German words are spelled almost like English words, differing only in one or two letters: **Amerika**, **Fisch**, **Kaffee**, **Prinz**. In these words and many others, English hard *c* becomes German **k**, English *sh* becomes German **sch**, and English soft *c* becomes German **z**. Some other German cognates have two dots — called Umlaut — over the vowels **a**, **o**, and **u**. This Umlaut changes the pronunciation of the vowel: **Bäcker** = *baker*, **Öl** = *oil*, **grün** = *green*.

How many of the following German words can you understand? Fill the blanks with their English meanings. If you need to, you may look in a dictionary:

1. Amerika	________________	**11.** Eisberg	________________
2. Appetit	________________	**12.** elegant	________________
3. Armee	________________	**13.** Ende	________________
4. Asche	________________	**14.** Energie	________________
5. Bäcker	________________	**15.** Familie	________________
6. Banane	________________	**16.** Fingernagel	________________
7. blond	________________	**17.** Fisch	________________
8. braun	________________	**18.** Garten	________________
9. Busch	________________	**19.** Gras	________________
10. Diamant	________________	**20.** Haar	________________

21. Haus ____________________

22. hundert ____________________

23. Ingenieur ____________________

24. Insekt ____________________

25. Januar ____________________

26. Juli ____________________

27. Juni ____________________

28. jung ____________________

29. Kaffee ____________________

30. Klasse ____________________

31. Konzert ____________________

32. Korn ____________________

33. Krokodil ____________________

34. Lampe ____________________

35. laut ____________________

36. Lippe ____________________

37. Mai ____________________

38. Mann ____________________

39. Maschine ____________________

40. Mathematik ____________________

41. Maus ____________________

42. Milch ____________________

43. Musik ____________________

44. Nummer ____________________

45. Offizier ____________________

46. Polizei ____________________

47. Prinz ____________________

48. rund ____________________

49. Schuh ____________________

50. Spanisch ____________________

3 German Names

Now that you are able to recognize over 50 German words resembling English, let's look at how German and English names compare.

Udo is going to help you learn how to pronounce some of these names.

You will meet **Udo** throughout this book holding his lens over one or two pronunciation clues he wants to share with you as you develop a good German pronunciation.

Whenever you look at **Udo's** clues, keep this in mind: every time you try to pronounce a German sound, hold your mouth, tongue, lips, and teeth in the same position at the end of the sound as you did at the beginning. Try saying **o** this way. Now try **oooo**. Again, try saying **u** this way. Now try **uuuu**. There, you've got it.

Udo has two clues for you before you listen to the following list of boys' and girls' names. The first one tells you how to pronounce HIS name:

The second clue tells you how to pronounce the German **r**.

Bruno

braun, rund

Here is a list of boys' and girls' names. With your teacher's help, choose a German name that you would like to have for yourself while you are studying German:

Alois
Anton
Augustin
Bernd
Boris
Bruno
Christian
Daniel
Dieter
Dirk
Edgar
Emil
Fritz
Günther
Hans
Heinz
Helmut
Herbert
Jens
Johann
Jürgen
Karl
Klaus
Konrad
Kurt
Lars
Leopold
Ludwig
Michael
Oskar
Otto
Richard
Rudi
Thomas
Udo
Viktor
Wolfgang

Agnes
Andrea
Annemarie
Brigitte
Christine
Claudia
Erika
Gisela
Gretel
Heidi
Heike
Helga
Hilde
Ilse
Inge
Ingrid
Jutta
Karin
Klara
Lotte
Luise
Magda
Margot
Maria
Marianne
Marlene
Monika
Olga
Petra
Renate
Sabine
Silke
Stefanie
Susanne
Ulrike

ÜBUNG

When Germans want to say, "My name is Heinrich," they say, **"Ich heiße Heinrich."** Practice telling your teacher and your classmates your name in German. If you and your teacher have chosen German names, use them.

Hans, Karin

Dialog 1 *Guten Tag*

* **du** means you in German; **du** is used when you are speaking to a close relative, a friend, or a child — someone with whom you are familiar. To say *you*, the Germans also use **Sie** when speaking to a stranger or a grown-up — a person with whom you should be formal. The exercises in this book use **du**.

ÜBUNG

Now let's review what you learned in Dialog 1:

1. Guten Tag, ____________________ (name).

Guten Tag, ____________________ (name).

2. Wie heißt du?

Ich heiße ____________________. Und du? Wie heißt du?

3. Freut mich, ____________________ (name).

Freut mich auch, ____________________ (name).

4. Auf Wiedersehen!

Auf Wiedersehen!

Kulturwinkel

Greetings!

Germans customarily shake hands more frequently than Americans when they greet each other. People usually shake hands every time they meet and every time they part. Except for close relatives, it is not common in Germany to kiss women on the cheek. But it is still customary in Germany for a man to remove his hat or cap when greeting a woman.

Here are some common German greetings:

Tag!	Hi!, Hello! (informal)
Guten Tag!	Hello!, Good day! (formal)
Guten Morgen!	Good morning!
Guten Abend!	Good evening!
Gute Nacht!	Good night!
(Auf) Wiedersehen!	Good-bye!
Tschüs!	Bye-bye!, So long!

4 Numbers

z**e**hn, s**i**eben

You will soon be able to count to forty in German. Listen to your teacher or the cassette to learn how to say the numbers 1 to 20.

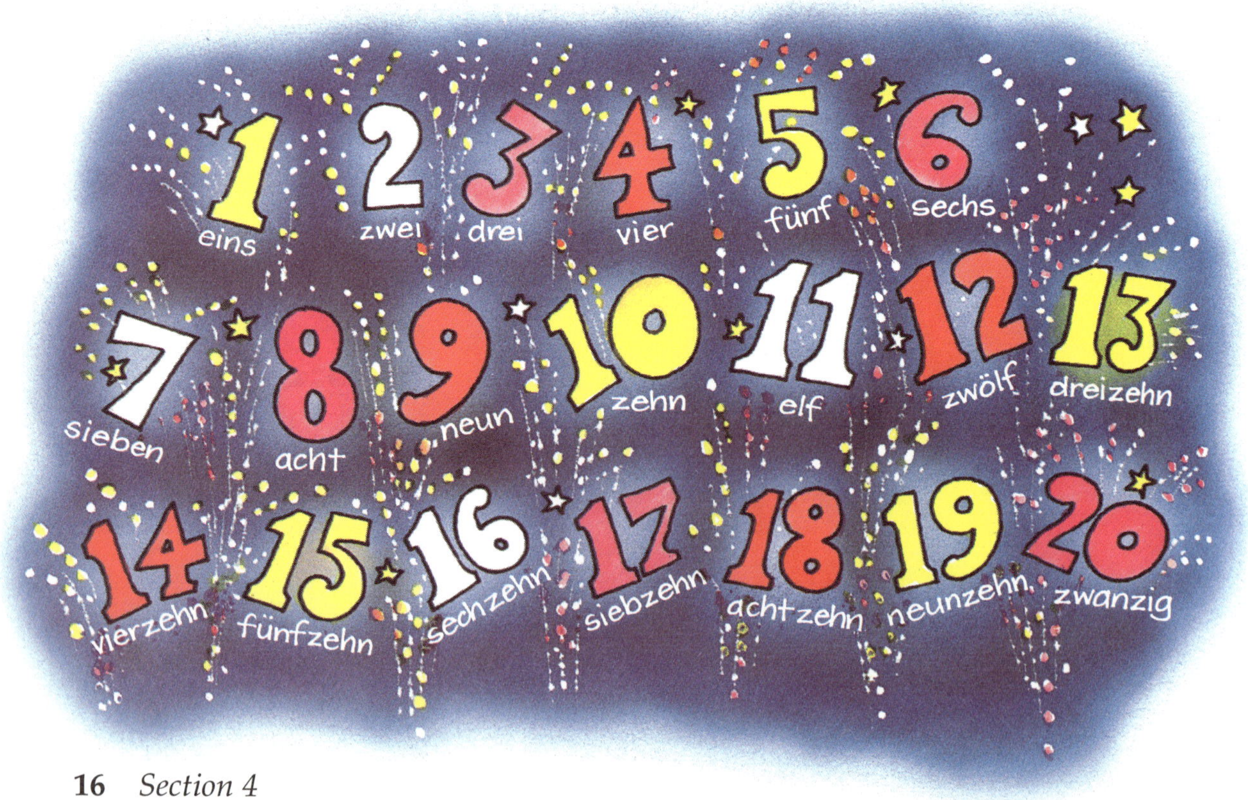

1 eins
2 zwei
3 drei
4 vier
5 fünf
6 sechs
7 sieben
8 acht
9 neun
10 zehn
11 elf
12 zwölf
13 dreizehn
14 vierzehn
15 fünfzehn
16 sechzehn
17 siebzehn
18 achtzehn
19 neunzehn
20 zwanzig

ÜBUNG

1. Cover page 16 with a sheet of paper. Then cover the German number words below and say the numbers aloud in German.

2. Now cover the German number words and write the German number words in the blank lines.

siebzehn	________	17	fünfzehn	________	15
acht	________	8	sechzehn	________	16
drei	________	3	sieben	________	7
eins	________	1	vier	________	4
neun	________	9	achtzehn	________	18
elf	________	11	zwölf	________	12
dreizehn	________	13	vierzehn	________	14
fünf	________	5	zehn	________	10
neunzehn	________	19	zwanzig	________	20
sechs	________	6	zwei	________	2

3. Pretend you are the teacher and correct your work with a red pen or pencil. You will be able to see at a glance which words you need to study further.

ÜBUNG

Your teacher will read some German numbers to you. Write the numerals for the number you hear:

1. ________ **4.** ________ **7.** ________ **10.** ________

2. ________ **5.** ________ **8.** ________ **11.** ________

3. ________ **6.** ________ **9.** ________ **12.** ________

Let's continue learning numbers. Listen to your teacher or the cassette to learn how to say the numbers 21 to 40.

ÜBUNG

Cover the top of page 18 with a sheet of paper while you do the next three activities. Your teacher will read some numbers from 21 to 40 in random order to you. Write the numerals for the German number you hear:

1. ______________________
2. ______________________
3. ______________________
4. ______________________
5. ______________________
6. ______________________
7. ______________________
8. ______________________
9. ______________________
10. ______________________

See how many German number words you can recognize. Draw a line to match the German number word with its numeral:

sechsundzwanzig	32
zweiunddreißig	29
dreiundzwanzig	21
vierunddreißig	28
neunundzwanzig	34
vierzig	40
sechsunddreißig	26
achtundzwanzig	23
neununddreißig	36
einundzwanzig	39

ÜBUNG

Now your teacher will read some numbers in English. Write the number words in German:

1. ______________________ **6.** ______________________

2. ______________________ **7.** ______________________

3. ______________________ **8.** ______________________

4. ______________________ **9.** ______________________

5. ______________________ **10.** ______________________

ÜBUNG

Now that you know the numbers from 1 to 40, let's try some math. First let's look at some words you will need to know:

Now write the answers to the following arithmetic problems in German. Then find the correct answers in the puzzle. Circle them from left to right, right to left, up or down, or diagonally:

1. zehn weniger sechs ist ______________
2. achtzehn und sechs ist ______________
3. dreizehn weniger drei ist ______________
4. zehn und zehn ist ______________
5. acht und sechs ist ______________
6. eins und sieben ist ______________
7. fünfzehn weniger zwei ist ______________
8. acht und acht ist ______________
9. zehn und zwei ist ______________
10. zwölf und sechs ist ______________
11. vierzig weniger achtunddreißig ist ______________
12. sieben weniger vier ist ______________

13. fünfzehn weniger zehn ist ________________

14. dreißig weniger neunzehn ist ________________

15. sechzehn weniger neun ist ________________

16. dreizehn und zwei ist ________________

17. neun und acht ist ________________

18. zwanzig weniger eins ist ________________

19. sechs und drei ist ________________

20. vierzig weniger elf ist ________________

I N N H E Z F N U F Z I G S Q
C P U V T V I E R Z E H N I D
F O F U I R Q L F E H N E E R
M S N H L E P F G M N H U B E
N T U P O Z R I Y I T E N E I
H Q F I E W Z O E N X Z S N Z
E Z L K J N A R P S I H O R E
Z T H C A E D E B D A C E I H
B K Z W O L F N E Z I E R O N
E J Z N E U N Z E H N S H W Y
I A C H T Z E H N A H B M G O
S V I E R U N D Z W A N Z I G
J N E U N U N D Z W A N Z I G

5 Days of the Week

Udo's clue:

Vowels with Umlaut do not exist in English.

- Pronounce **ä** like *e* in *bed*.
- For **ö**, round your lips for *o* in *rope* and pronounce *e* in *they*.
- For **ü**, round your lips as if about to whistle and pronounce *ee* in *meet*.

M**ä**rz, **Ö**l, f**ü**nf

NOVEMBER

MONTAG	DIENSTAG	MITTWOCH	DONNERSTAG	FREITAG	SAMSTAG	SONNTAG
1	2	3	4	5	6	7
8	9	10	11	12	13	14
15	16	17	18	19	20	21
22	23	24	25	26	27	28
29	30	31				

These are the days of the week in German. The German week begins with Monday.

Heute ist Montag. = *Today is Monday.*

Each day, find as many people as you can and tell them the day of the week in German.

Kulturwinkel In der Schule (At school)

Complete the following school schedule with the subjects you are taking this year:

	MONTAG	DIENSTAG	MITTWOCH	DONNERSTAG	FREITAG

Now look at a typical schedule of a German student. Compare it with yours. What are the differences? What are the similarities?

	MONTAG	DIENSTAG	MITTWOCH	DONNERSTAG	FREITAG	SAMSTAG
8.00 – 8.45	Math	German	English	Math	German	Religion
8.45 – 9.30	History	Biology	English	German	Biology	History
9.30 – 10.15	English	Art	History	Social Studies	Math	Geography
10.40 – 11.25	Social Studies	Music	Religion	Latin	English	
11.25 – 12.10	Sports	Latin	Art	Geography	Needlework	
12.20 – 13.05	Sports	Needlework	Sports	Music	Sports	

There are usually short pauses between classes, and students normally stay in the same room for most classes. A longer recess (**Große Pause**) from 10:15 to 10:40 provides time for socializing and a mid-morning snack. The short recess (**Kleine Pause**) from 12:10 to 12:20 gives students some additional free time.

Parents of German students receive periodic report cards. Grades range from 1 to 6. Most students want an **"Eins"** (1), the highest grade. A grade of 5 or 6 is unsatisfactory.

What other differences can you see between American and German school days?

6 Months of the Year

The months of the year in German resemble English. Can you recognize all of them?

ÜBUNG

Unscramble the letters to form the name of a German month:

1. B R E A F U R
2. P R A I L
3. B R E E N V O M
4. A I M
5. N U J I
6. Z R A M
7. B E Z E D R E M
8. S U G A T U
9. U J I L
10. T O B K E R O
11. N A U R A J
12. T E S M P R E B E

Match the names of the months with their numbers by drawing lines between the two columns. For example, January is number one and December is number twelve:

März	sieben
September	fünf
Juli	drei
Januar	vier
Dezember	zehn
August	zwei
April	neun
Oktober	zwölf
Februar	sechs
Mai	eins
November	acht
Juni	elf

ÜBUNG

Answer the following questions with the German months:

1. Which is your favorite month?

____

2. Which is your least favorite month?

____

3. In which month is your birthday?

____

4. In which month does your mother celebrate her birthday?

____

5. In which month does your father celebrate his birthday?

____

6. In which month does your best friend celebrate her/his birthday? ______________________________

7. When does your teacher celebrate her/his birthday?

____

8. In which months do you have vacation?

____

Fill in the blanks with the correct German names of the days or months, then find the nineteen days or months in the puzzle. Circle them from left to right, right to left, up or down, or diagonally:

1. The day after Monday: ____________________

2. The day before Thursday: ____________________

3. The first day of the weekend: ____________________

4. Garfield hates this day: ____________________

5. Many people go to church on this day of the week: ____________________

6. The day before Friday: ____________________

7. The last day of your school week: ____________________

8. The first month of the year: ____________________

9. The month of Christmas: ____________________

10. The month of Thanksgiving: ____________________

11. The month you go back to school after the summer break: ____________________

12. Halloween is on the last day of this month: ____________________

13. The month of the United States' birthday: ____________________

14. Memorial Day occurs toward the end of this month: ____________________

15. The month of St. Patrick's day: ____________________

16. Flag Day is celebrated in this month: ______________________

17. The month of Valentine's Day: ______________________

18. The month after July: ______________________

19. April Fool's Day is the first day of this month: ______________________

O	K	T	O	B	E	R	A	C	T	S	U	G	U	A
S	D	M	U	J	U	N	I	A	S	U	V	P	Q	R
T	I	G	R	O	A	P	R	I	L	O	N	U	E	N
D	E	G	L	E	P	N	A	G	A	T	S	M	A	S
O	N	T	A	Q	B	P	U	C	P	B	A	Q	L	O
N	S	G	O	T	O	M	N	A	M	E	H	E	B	N
N	T	L	U	J	S	I	E	P	R	L	C	F	G	N
E	A	N	A	H	W	N	S	Z	E	Z	O	D	N	T
R	G	J	U	L	I	X	E	L	E	M	W	R	N	A
S	J	J	K	H	G	F	U	I	V	D	T	L	O	G
T	F	E	B	R	U	A	R	H	O	I	T	B	S	E
A	D	I	Z	E	N	B	R	F	R	E	I	T	A	G
G	I	Q	I	G	A	T	N	O	M	O	M	A	R	Z
A	R	E	B	M	E	V	O	N	A	A	D	T	S	A
S	E	P	T	E	M	B	E	R	I	C	O	L	P	W

ÜBUNG

Now that you have learned the names of the days and months, let's learn how to say dates. When the Germans want to say, "Today is Monday, July fourteenth," they say, **"Heute ist Montag, der vierzehnte Juli."** "Today is Friday, March first" would be **"Heute ist Freitag, der erste März."**

German, like English, uses ordinal numbers in dates. Add **-te** for the numbers **zwei** to **neunzehn**, **-ste** for the numbers **zwanzig** and higher. There are three exceptions:

The first of the month is **der erste**.

The third of the month is **der dritte**.

The seventh of the month is **der siebte**.

Germans often write dates in figures followed by a period:

der 14. Juli = der vierzehnte Juli

der 1. März = der erste März

der 20. Mai = der zwanzigste Mai

If you want to express "on July fourteenth" in German, say **"am vierzehnten Juli."** Notice that an **n** is added to the number.

Now, your teacher will divide the class into small groups. Each of you will choose your birthday month and make up a calendar for that month. Complete the calendar with the days of the week and the month in German and enter the dates.

MONTAG						SONNTAG

Now that you have completed your calendar, take turns pointing to several dates and saying them to your partners. Then point to the date of your birthdate and say: **Mein Geburtstag ist am** *(My birthday is [on])* . . . followed by the date, with the number ending in **n**.

Dialog 2 *Was ist das?*

* German nouns, or names of objects, are masculine, feminine, or neuter. German has two words meaning *a, an:* **ein** is used with masculine and neuter nouns and **eine** is used with feminine nouns.

ÜBUNG

Now let's review what you learned in Dialog 2:

1. Tag, ________________ (name)!

2. Wie geht's?

Sehr gut, danke.

3. Was ist das?

Das ist ein(e) ________________.

4. Danke.

Bitteschön.

Kulturwinkel

German Holidays

Most legal holidays celebrated in Germany are based on the religious calendar and are similar to holidays we observe in the United States:

Christmas ***(Weihnachten)*****:** The holiday begins with Christmas Eve on December 24 and continues for two days on December 25 and 26. Germans celebrate by exchanging gifts and decorating the Christmas tree ***(der Weihnachtsbaum)***. Students enjoy two weeks vacation until after the New Year holiday.

New Year ***(Neujahr)*****:** New Year's Eve is called ***Silvester***. As midnight approaches, church bells ring all over Germany.

Carnival ***(Karneval)*****:** This holiday is celebrated mainly in Catholic areas. Cities known for their carnivals are Cologne, Mainz, and Munich, where people dress in costumes, hold parades, and have parties. The Carnival season reaches its high point just before Ash Wednesday, the beginning of Lent.

Easter *(Ostern)*: The Easter holiday is celebrated for two days. The coloring of Easter eggs, which are then hidden for children to find, is still a popular custom in Germany.

Labor Day *(Tag der Arbeit)*: May 1, formerly celebrated as May Day, is now dedicated to workers, who get a day off from work. Schools, of course, are also closed. In some areas, there are parades and dancing around the maypole.

German Unification Day *(Tag der deutschen Einheit)*: This relatively new holiday celebrates the 1990 unification of West and East Germany on October 3.

Pentecost *(Pfingsten)*: This two-day holiday occurs seven weeks after Easter and is traditionally celebrated with family outings.

Other holidays are celebrated regionally, such as the ***Oktoberfest*** in Munich, wine festivals in the wine areas along the Rhine and Mosel Rivers, and harvest festivals in many towns and villages throughout Germany.

7 The Classroom

Udo's clues:

a**ch**t, Bu**ch**, au**ch**

i**ch**, Mäd**ch**en, se**ch**zehn

ja, **J**unge, **J**uli

Learn the names of the objects in your classroom. See how many names you can remember at a time without having to look at the book.

ein Junge
ein Schüler
ein Stuhl
ein Heft
ein Kugelschreiber
ein Buch

eine Tafel
ein Fenster
eine Lehrerin
ein Stück Kreide
ein Lehrer
eine Tür
ein Papier
ein Mädchen
eine Schülerin
ein Tisch
ein Bleistift
ein Lehrertisch

ÜBUNG

1. Name aloud as many of the classroom words in German as you can remember. Study the words you did not remember.
2. Write the names of the illustrations in German in the first column of blank lines.
3. Correct your work. Give yourself one point for each correct answer.
4. Now cover the illustrations and write the English meanings of the German words in the second column of blank lines.
5. Correct your work. Give yourself one point for each correct answer.

	WRITE GERMAN WORDS HERE	WRITE ENGLISH WORDS HERE
1.	______________________	______________________
2.	______________________	______________________
3.	______________________	______________________
4.	______________________	______________________
5.	______________________	______________________

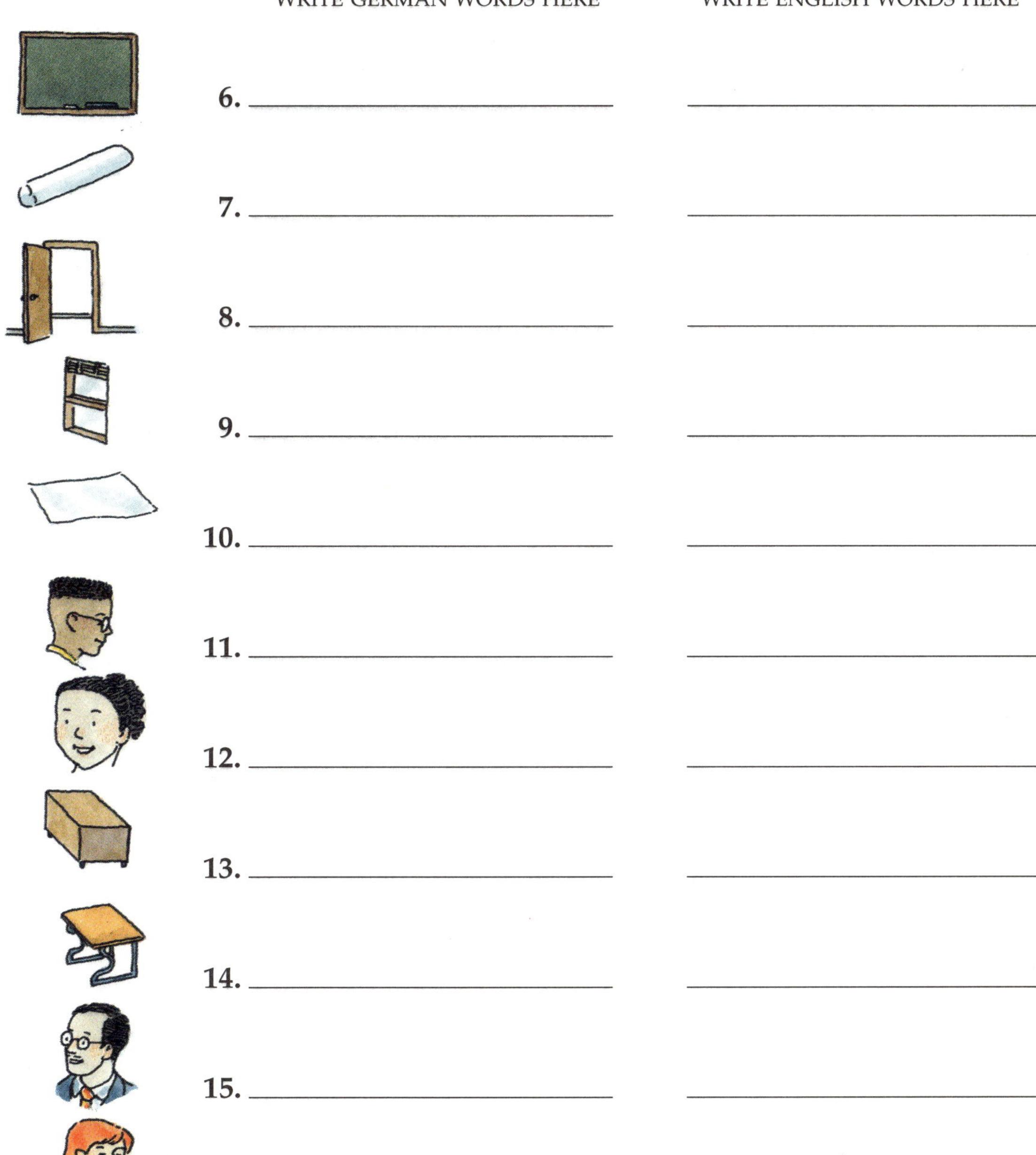

Thirty-two points is a perfect score. If you made a mistake, you can improve your score by repeating the exercise on a blank piece of paper and correcting it again.

Classroom Vocabulary Puzzle: To solve this puzzle, first express the following words in German, then fit them in the puzzle vertically and horizontally:

3-letter word

door ___ ___ ___

4-letter words

book ___ ___ ___ ___

notebook ___ ___ ___ ___

5-letter words

chalkboard ___ ___ ___ ___ ___

chair ___ ___ ___ ___ ___

boy ___ ___ ___ ___ ___

6-letter words

chalk ___ ___ ___ ___ ___ ___

paper ___ ___ ___ ___ ___ ___

7-letter words

girl ___ ___ ___ ___ ___ ___ ___

window ___ ___ ___ ___ ___ ___ ___

8-letter word

female teacher ___ ___ ___ ___ ___ ___ ___ ___

9-letter word

pencil ___ ___ ___ ___ ___ ___ ___ ___ ___

11-letter word

teacher's desk ___ ___ ___ ___ ___ ___ ___ ___ ___ ___ ___

14-letter word

pen ___ ___ ___ ___ ___ ___ ___ ___ ___ ___ ___ ___ ___ ___

Kulturwinkel

School and Leisure Time

Every German youngster attends kindergarten and then primary school for the first four grades. Starting with the fifth grade, German students can choose to attend different types of secondary schools leading either to academic or vocational studies. At the end of their studies, students must pass a special test to qualify for a place in the university.

German students attend school from Monday to Friday and in some schools on one Saturday a month. Most students take about a dozen subjects at a time, although, of course, not every subject is scheduled every day.

There are about six weeks of summer vacation. Vacation times are staggered in different states of the country to avoid excessive congestion on the highways. Schools are also closed for two to three weeks during the Christmas-New Year season and in the spring.

Young Germans enjoy many of the same leisure activities as their contemporaries in the United States: sports (soccer is by far the most popular sport in Germany), movies, music, arts and crafts, and above all family and school excursions. Germans are passionate travelers and can be seen in large numbers at all the popular travel spots, both in Germany itself as well as throughout Europe and more distant foreign countries.

1. Which classes, sports, and leisure activities are you involved in this year?

____

2. Do you participate in group excursions? If yes, where did you go this year?

____

____

8 Colors

Udo's clues:

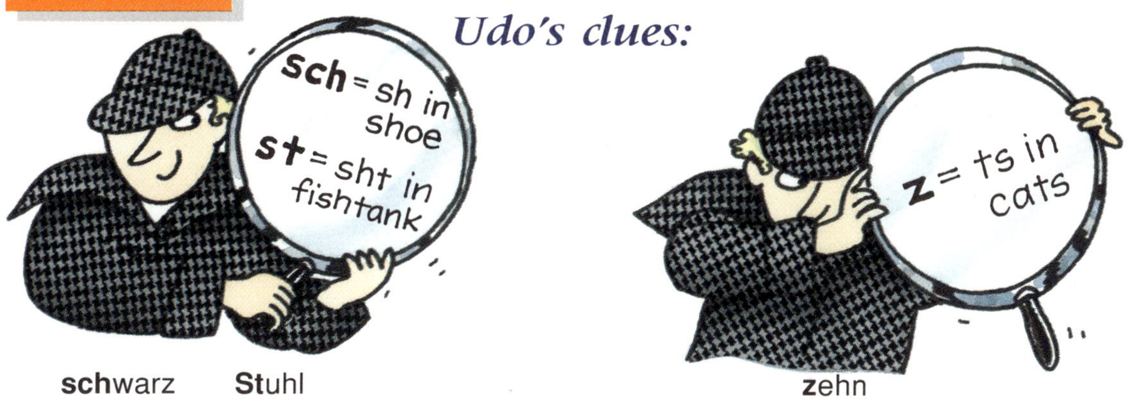

sch = sh in shoe
st = sht in fishtank

schwarz **St**uhl

z = ts in cats

zehn

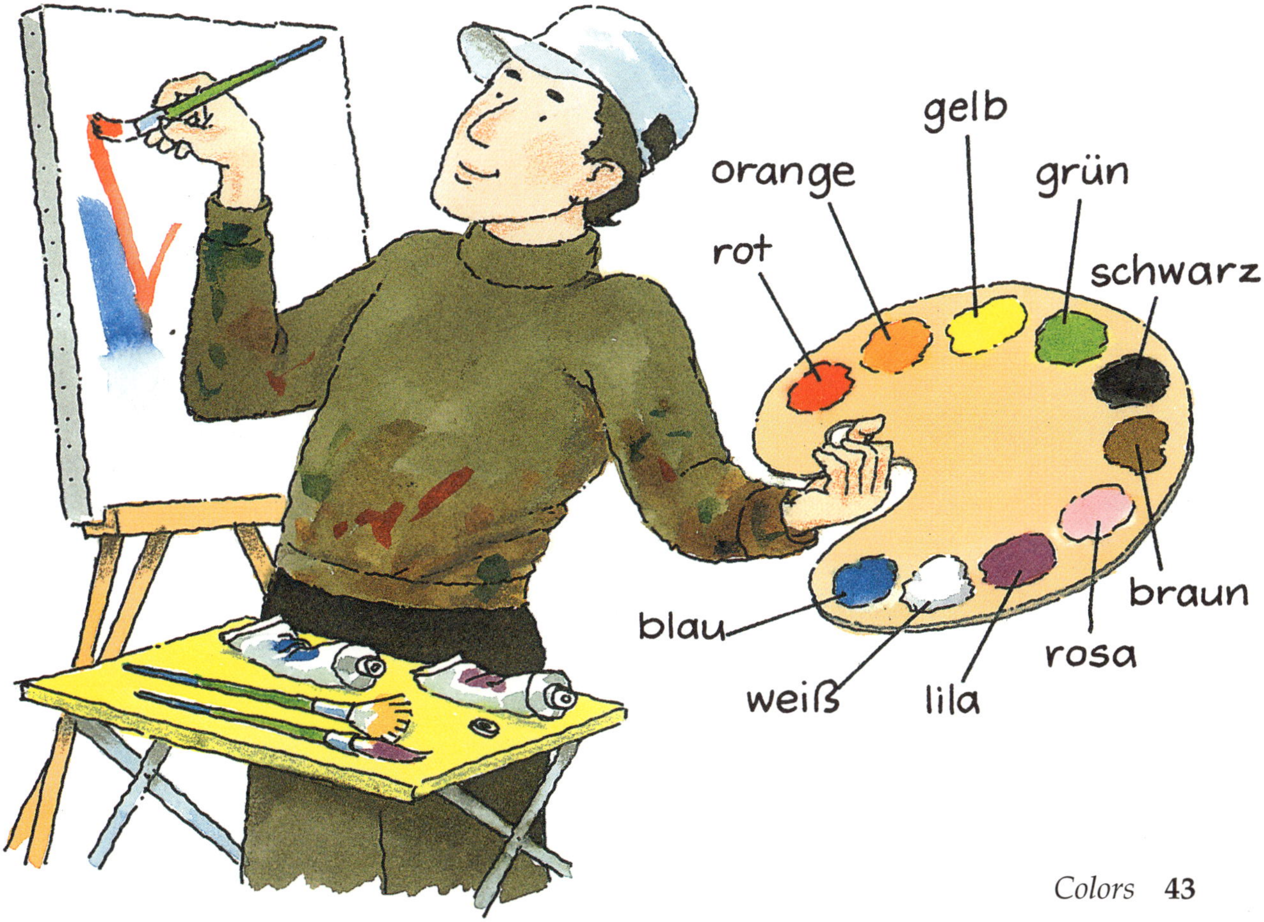
gelb
orange
grün
rot
schwarz
braun
blau
rosa
weiß
lila

ÜBUNG

How many German color words can you memorize in one minute? Two minutes? Five? When you feel ready, test yourself:

1. Say as many German color words as you can remember.
2. Write the German color words in the first column of blank lines.
3. Check your work and give yourself one point for each correct answer.
4. Now cover the colors and write the English meanings of the German color words in the second column of blank lines.
5. Check your work and give yourself one point for each correct answer.

	WRITE GERMAN WORDS HERE	WRITE ENGLISH WORDS HERE
1.	______________	______________
2.	______________	______________
3.	______________	______________
4.	______________	______________
5.	______________	______________
6.	______________	______________
7.	______________	______________
8.	______________	______________
9.	______________	______________
10.	______________	______________

Did you get 20 points? If not, try again with a blank piece of paper.

ÜBUNG

Here are pictures of items for which you have already learned the German names:

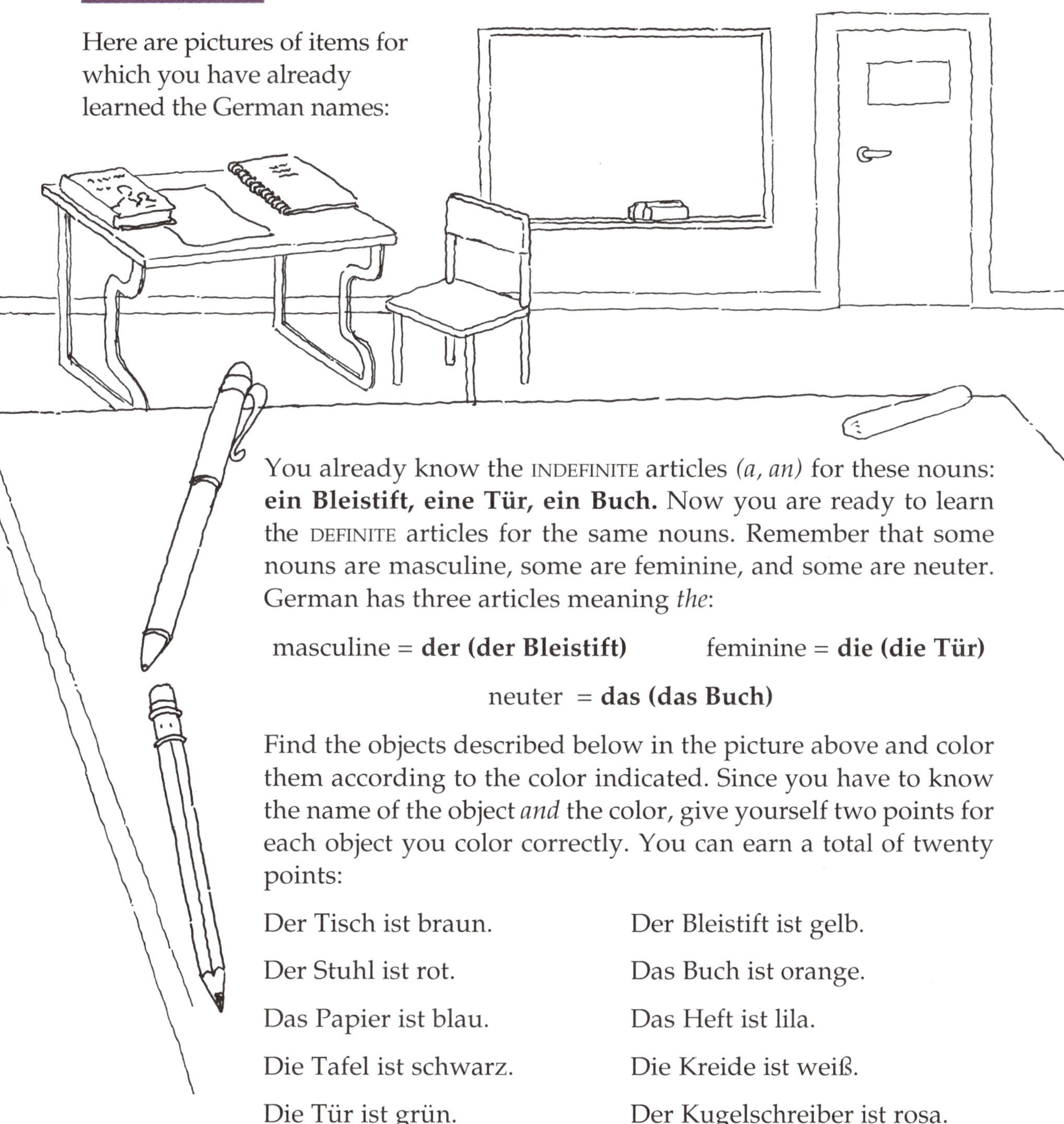

You already know the INDEFINITE articles *(a, an)* for these nouns: **ein Bleistift, eine Tür, ein Buch.** Now you are ready to learn the DEFINITE articles for the same nouns. Remember that some nouns are masculine, some are feminine, and some are neuter. German has three articles meaning *the*:

masculine = **der (der Bleistift)** feminine = **die (die Tür)**

neuter = **das (das Buch)**

Find the objects described below in the picture above and color them according to the color indicated. Since you have to know the name of the object *and* the color, give yourself two points for each object you color correctly. You can earn a total of twenty points:

Der Tisch ist braun.	Der Bleistift ist gelb.
Der Stuhl ist rot.	Das Buch ist orange.
Das Papier ist blau.	Das Heft ist lila.
Die Tafel ist schwarz.	Die Kreide ist weiß.
Die Tür ist grün.	Der Kugelschreiber ist rosa.

ÜBUNG

You've already seen this map. Color the countries where German is spoken according to the colors below:

Germany — **gelb**

Austria — **rot**

Switzerland — **blau**

Liechtenstein — **grün**

Luxemburg — **braun**

9 The Body

Udo's clues:

When you want to talk about yourself in German, you will need to know the names of the parts of the body. How many names can you remember without having to look at the book?

ÜBUNG

Fill in the names of the parts of the body:

ÜBUNG

Choose a partner. Point to each other's hand, foot, and so on, and ask, **"Was ist das?"** Answer, **"Das ist eine Hand," "Das ist ein Bein"** (or **"Das ist die Hand," "Das ist das Bein"**) and so on.

ÜBUNG

Complete this crossword puzzle with the German names of the parts of the body (in puzzles using capital letters, **ß** becomes **SS**):

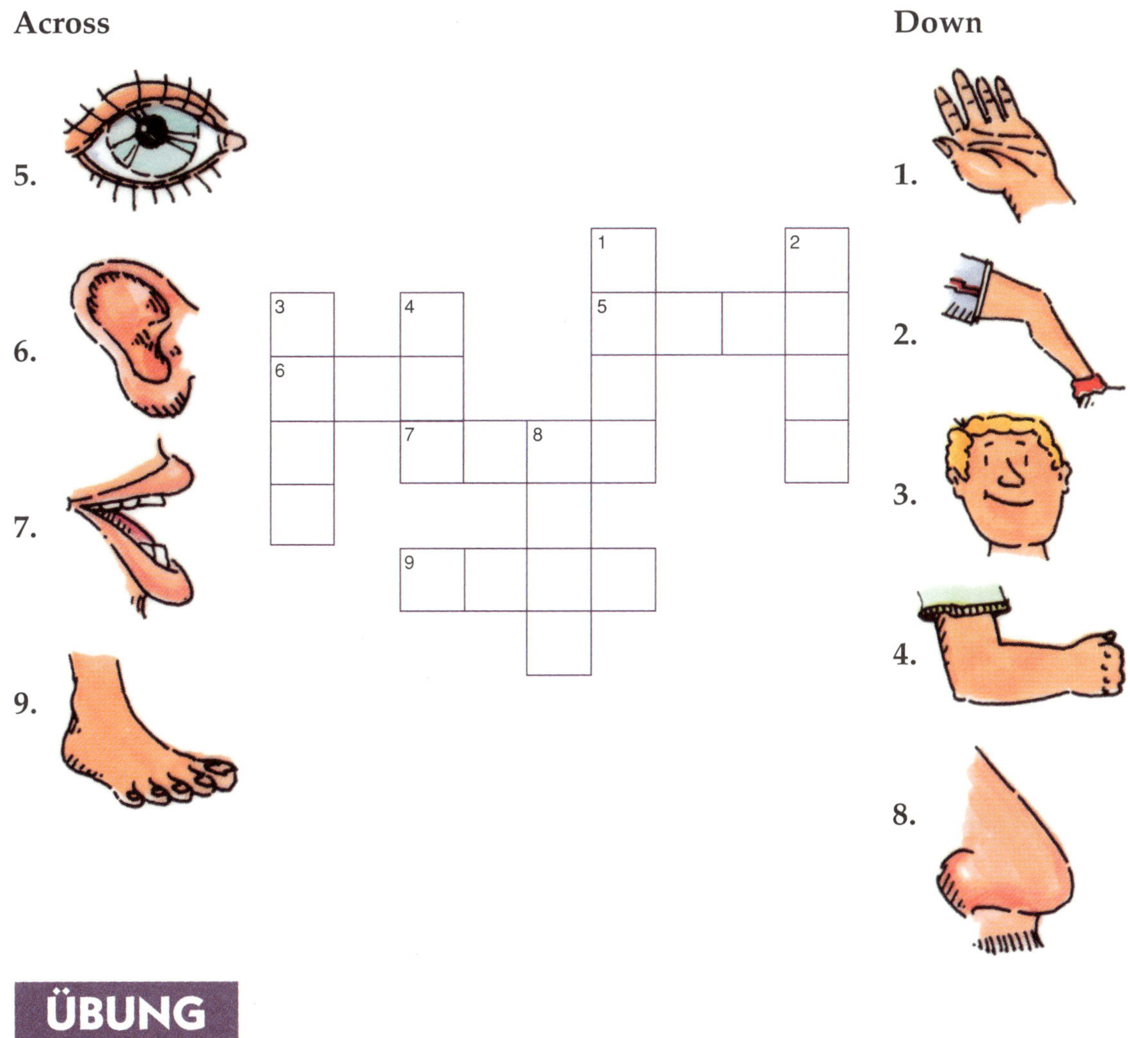

ÜBUNG

"Simon sagt" means *"Simon says."* Move or point to that part of the body Simon refers to only if you hear the words **"Simon sagt."** If you do not hear the words **"Simon sagt,"** don't move at all.

Kulturwinkel

Some Interesting German Manners and Customs

Germans eat by keeping the fork in the left hand and the knife in the right hand throughout a meal. Eating with knife and fork in this manner is also becoming more prevalent in the United States.

It is customary to bring something for your host or hostess if you're invited to a German home. A box of chocolates or a bouquet of flowers would be just fine. But don't forget to unwrap the flowers before you present them, for it is considered rude to offer flowers inside wrapping paper.

Germans are much more formal than Americans toward one another. That is why the German language has formal and familiar forms for ***you***. Family members, young people, and close friends say **du** to each other, but **Sie** is used for strangers, adults, and business associates. And while your teacher will say **du** to you (at least until you get to high school), good manners require that you address your teacher with **Sie**. A good rule to follow: When in doubt, use **Sie**.

Floors in German buildings are numbered beginning with the floor ABOVE the ground floor: **der erste Stock** (first floor) is our second floor, **der zweite Stock** (second floor) is our third floor, and so on. Keep these differences in mind when you shop in a German department store. The ground floor is called **das Erdgeschoß** (literally, earth floor).

der dritte Stock

der zweite Stock

der erste Stock

das Erdgeschoß

Speaking of shopping in Germany, expect to see labels like these:

These labels look a little strange because Germans use a comma where Americans use a decimal point. As you might have guessed, the reverse is also true: Germans use a decimal point where Americans use a comma:

(Germany) **2.350,25** = (U.S.A.) **2,350.25**

While Americans in general do their grocery shopping once a week, many Germans prefer to buy fresh meats, produce, and baked goods every day for their meals. By the way, the main meal in Germany is still usually eaten at midday.

10 Talking About Yourself

An adjective describes a person or thing. In the sentence "The beautiful girl is happy," *beautiful* and *happy* are adjectives that describe *girl*. Many adjectives are easy to remember if you think of them in pairs:

ÜBUNG

Cover page 52 with a sheet of paper and write the German adjectives that describe the objects you see:

1. ____________________ 2. ____________________ 3. ____________________

4. ____________________ 5. ____________________ 6. ____________________

7. ____________________ 8. ____________________ 9. ____________________

10. ____________________ 11. ____________________ 12. ____________________

Dialog 3 *Ich bin . . .*

Aber nein,
du bist
intelligent.
Und schön?
Ja, du bist auch schön.
Und stark,
ich bin
stark?
Ja, du bist auch stark.
Ja, ich bin
intelligent, stark
und schön.
Danke, Karin.
Ich bin jetzt glücklich.
Tschüs, Karin!
Tschüs,
Hans!

Let's take a closer look at some of the words you learned in Dialog 3:

Ich bin . . .

Du bist . . .

Er ist . . .
Der Junge ist . . .

Sie ist . . .
Das Mädchen ist . . .

ÜBUNG

Your teacher will now divide you into small groups to practice describing yourself and one another.

ÜBUNG

Play charades with the adjectives you have learned. Your teacher will divide the class into teams, and a member from one team will stand in front of the class and act out the various ways he or she would look if sad, intelligent, fat, and so on.

Kulturwinkel

Sports in Germany

Fußball *(Soccer)* is not only the most popular spectator sport in Germany but also the sport that young Germans most actively engage in as soon as they are old enough to kick a soccer ball. Every school and every town has its own soccer team, and the national team is followed by practically every German whenever it plays an international match.

Germans of all ages are also actively engaged in a variety of other individual and team sports: tennis, gymnastics, track and field, swimming, bicycling, and skiing. In recent years, basketball and volleyball have become increasingly popular, but American football and baseball are still relatively rare.

11 The Family

Here we have a typical German family **(die Familie)**. Let's take a closer look at the family members:

Naturally, German boys and girls also use nicknames for their parents and grandparents:

der Vati = der Vater **die Mutti = die Mutter**

der Opa = der Großvater **die Oma = die Großmutter**

If you want to say "my father," "my mother," "your father," "your mother," it's really very simple:

mein Vater **meine Mutter**

dein Vater **deine Mutter**

Use **mein / dein** for masculine and **meine / deine** for feminine.

ÜBUNG

Wer ist das? Identify these members of the family. Use nicknames, if you like. Here's an example:

Das ist die Mutti.

Now it's your turn. **Wer ist das?**

1. ____________________
   ____

2. ____________________
   ____

3. ____________________
   ____

4. ____________________
   ____

5. ____________________
   ____

ÜBUNG

Team up with a partner in the following dialog. Make believe that you are describing a member of your partner's family, but your partner responds with the opposite description. Here's an example to get you started:

You	Your Partner
Dein Großvater ist klein.	Nein, mein Großvater ist groß.
1. ______________________	______________________
2. ______________________	______________________
3. ______________________	______________________
4. ______________________	______________________

12 Recycling German

Your teacher will now give you time to use your German. Think of all you have learned!

- You can say your name!
- You can count and do math!
- You can name the days of the week and the months of the year!
- You can name objects in the classroom with their colors!
- You can describe yourself and others and point out parts of the body!

When someone asks if you can speak German: **Sprichst du Deutsch?**, now you can answer: **Ja, ich spreche Deutsch!**

ÜBUNG

Fill in the boxes with the German meanings and you will find a mystery word in the longest vertical column. Write the mystery word in German and English in the blanks provided:

1. three
2. Monday
3. January
4. boy
5. desk
6. ear
7. window
8. red
9. thank you
10. pen

____

____

Colors: What would this funny monster look like if you could color the parts of its body? Write the names of the parts of the body and the colors you would choose in the blanks below. Then color the parts of the body in the picture:

	Part of the body	**Color**
1.	____________________	____________________
2.	____________________	____________________
3.	____________________	____________________
4.	____________________	____________________
5.	____________________	____________________
6.	____________________	____________________
7.	____________________	____________________
8.	____________________	____________________
9.	____________________	____________________

ÜBUNG

Can you complete these dialogs or express the following ideas in German?

1. You overhear the conversation of these two people who are meeting for the first time. Complete the dialog:

2. Peter is teaching some German words to his little brother. Complete the dialog:

3. What do you think these friends are saying to each other?

4. What are the colors of the American flag?

_______________ _______________ _______________

5. What are the names of these parts of the body?

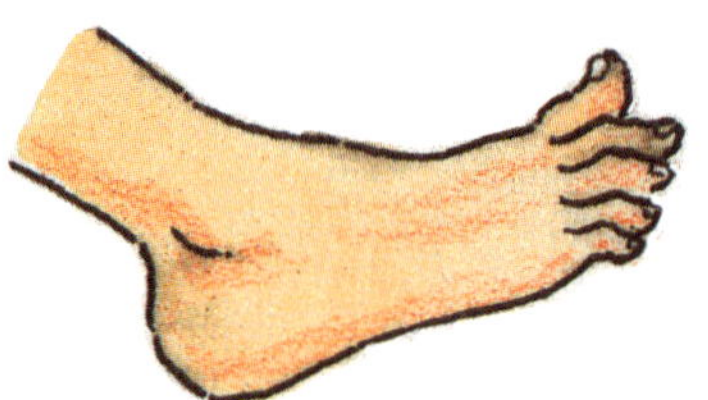

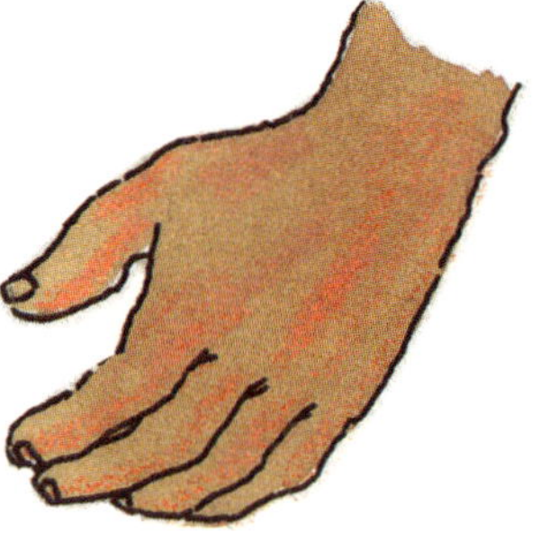

_______________ _______________ _______________

6. What days of the week are missing from this agenda?

7. What month is it?

______________________ ______________________ ______________________

8. What adjectives describe these people?

______________________ ______________________ ______________________

ÜBUNG

This game is played like **Bingo,** except that it is played with words. Select German words from the categories in the vocabulary list on pages 70 to 73 as directed by your teacher. Write one word in each square at random from the chosen categories.

Your teacher will read the **Bingo** words in English. If one of the German words on your card matches the English word you hear, mark that square with a small star. When you have five stars in a row, either horizontally, vertically, or diagonally, call out **"Bingo!"**

Kulturwinkel

Hurrah for the differences!

Now that you have learned quite a bit about the German language and about Germany and its people, can you list the differences between Germans and Americans that impressed you the most? Jog your memory by looking over the **Kulturwinkel** on pages 15, 23, 34–35, 42, 50–51, and 58.

An example is given to get you started:

	GERMAN	AMERICAN
1.	*Friends and relatives greet each other with "Tag" and shake hands.*	*Friends and relatives say "Hi" and may kiss women on the cheek.*
2.	______________________	______________________
3.	______________________	______________________
4.	______________________	______________________
5.	______________________	______________________
6.	______________________	______________________

Vocabulary

Numbers

eins	1
zwei	2
drei	3
vier	4
fünf	5
sechs	6
sieben	7
acht	8
neun	9
zehn	10
elf	11
zwölf	12
dreizehn	13
vierzehn	14
fünfzehn	15
sechzehn	16
siebzehn	17
achtzehn	18
neunzehn	19
zwanzig	20
einundzwanzig	21
zweiundzwanzig	22
dreiundzwanzig	23
vierundzwanzig	24
fünfundzwanzig	25
sechsundzwanzig	26
siebenundzwanzig	27
achtundzwanzig	28
neunundzwanzig	29
dreißig	30
einunddreißig	31
zweiunddreißig	32
dreiunddreißig	33
vierunddreißig	34
fünfunddreißig	35
sechsunddreißig	36
siebenunddreißig	37
achtunddreißig	38
neununddreißig	39
vierzig	40

Arithmetic

Wie viele?	How many?
ist	equals
und	and, plus
weniger	minus

Days of the week

Montag	Monday
Dienstag	Tuesday
Mittwoch	Wednesday
Donnerstag	Thursday
Freitag	Friday
Samstag	Saturday
Sonntag	Sunday

Months of the year

Januar	January
Februar	February
März	March
April	April
Mai	May
Juni	June
Juli	July
August	August
September	September
Oktober	October
November	November
Dezember	December

The Classroom

ein Bleistift	a pencil
ein Buch	a book
ein Fenster	a window
ein Heft	a notebook
ein Junge	a boy
ein Kugelschreiber	a ballpoint pen
ein Lehrer	a (male) teacher
eine Lehrerin	a (female) teacher
ein Lehrertisch	a (teacher's) desk
ein Mädchen	a girl
ein Papier	a paper
ein Schüler	a (male) student
eine Schülerin	a (female) student
ein Stück Kreide	a piece of chalk
ein Stuhl	a chair
eine Tafel	a chalkboard
ein Tisch	a (student's) desk
eine Tür	a door

Colors

blau	blue
braun	brown
gelb	yellow
grün	green
lila	purple
orange	orange
rosa	pink
rot	red
schwarz	black
weiß	white

The Body

der Arm	the arm
das Auge	the eye
das Bein	the leg
der Fuß	the foot
die Hand	the hand
der Kopf	the head
der Mund	the mouth
die Nase	the nose
das Ohr	the ear

Adjectives

dein, deine	your
dick	fat
dumm	stupid, dumb
dünn	thin
glücklich	happy
groß	big, tall
häßlich	ugly
intelligent	intelligent, smart
klein	small
mein, meine	my
schön	beautiful, handsome
schwach	weak
stark	strong
traurig	sad

The Family

mein, meine	my
dein, deine	your
der Vater, der Vati	the father, the dad
die Mutter, die Mutti	the mother, the mom
der Großvater, der Opa	the grandfather
die Großmutter, die Oma	the grandmother
der Sohn	the son
die Tochter	the daughter
der Bruder	the brother
die Schwester	the sister

Expressions and phrases

Wie heißt du? / **Wie heißen Sie?**	What's your name?
Ich heiße . . .	My name is . . .
Und du?	And you?
Freut mich.	It's a pleasure.
Frau	Mrs., Ms.
Herr	Mister, sir
Tag!	Hi!, Hello! (informal)
Guten Tag!	Hello!, Good day! (formal)
Guten Morgen!	Good morning!
Guten Abend!	Good evening!
Gute Nacht!	Good night!
(Auf) Wiedersehen!	Good-bye!
Tschüs!	Bye-bye!, So long!
Heute ist (date).	Today is (date).
der erste	the first
der dritte	the third
der siebte	the seventh
der vierzehnte	the fourteenth
der zwanzigste	the twentieth
am vierzehnten	on the fourteenth

Mein Geburtstag ist am . . .	My birthday is [on] . . .
Wie geht's?	How are you?
Sehr gut, danke.	Very well, thank you.
Wer ist das?	Who is that?
Was ist das?	What is that?
Das ist ein(e) . . .	That is a (an) . . .
Das ist der (die, das) . . .	That is the . . .
Danke.	Thank you.
Bitteschön.	You're welcome.
Warum?	Why?
das Erdgeschoß	the ground floor
der erste Stock	the first floor
der zweite Stock	the second floor
der dritte Stock	the third floor
Ich bin . . .	I am . . .
Du bist . . .	You are . . .
Er ist . . .	He is . . .
Der Junge ist . . .	The boy is . . .
Sie ist . . .	She is . . .
Das Mädchen ist . . .	The girl is . . .
Sprichst du Deutsch?	Do you speak German?
Ja, ich spreche Deutsch.	Yes, I speak German.
Kulturwinkel	Culture corner
aber	but
auch	also
jetzt	now
und	and
Ja.	Yes.
Nein.	No.